SHAKESPEARE'S THEATRE AND THE DRAMATIC TRADITION

Shakespeare's Theatre and the Dramatic Tradition

BY LOUIS B. WRIGHT

FOLGER BOOKS

Published by
THE FOLGER SHAKESPEARE LIBRARY

First printing 1958
Second printing 1961
Third printing 1963
Fourth printing 1966
Fifth printing 1969
Sixth printing 1979

LC 79-65978

ISBN 0-918016-05-3

ISBN 0-918016-18-5 (Series)

Printed in the United States of America

FOR many years the characteristics of Shakespeare's stage have excited the interest of scholars. In thousands of pages of learned commentary they have discussed the history of Elizabethan theatres, the physical conditions of the stage, the composition of the companies of actors, the influence of the physical nature of the stage upon the quality of the drama, and scores of related topics. In an area where precise documentary evidence is scanty, many topics have aroused controversies that cannot be resolved dogmatically. For example, blueprints for the original construction of the Globe playhouse do not exist, and our knowledge of it is based on a variety of evidence, much of which is inconclusive.

Though scholars may not agree on every detail of stage construction, they have accumulated enough evidence to permit the reconstruction of a characteristic theatre in its essential outlines. The public theatres were not exact replicas of each other, of course, and the so-called "private" theatres showed many differences. We would do well to remember that, then as now, individual theatres varied considerably in their appointments and equipment, and a generalization about the staging of a play in one theatre may not precisely fit conditions in another. Nevertheless the conditions of staging in all of the public playhouses had a general similarity and certain theatrical practices were common to them all.

Traditionally the English had found pleasure and delight in

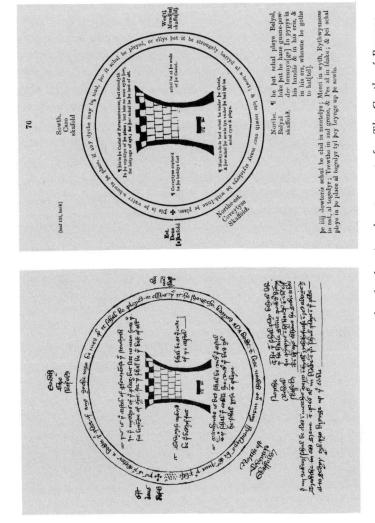

Plate 1. (Left) A fifteenth-century sketch showing the stage sets for *The Castle of Perseverance*. From a manuscript in the Folger Library. *(Right)* Manuscript notes of *The Castle of Perseverance* sketch reproduced in type.

dramatic entertainment. For centuries before the development of Elizabethan drama, folk games, pageantry, and processions had been a part of English life. Wandering entertainers had been a familiar sight in both manor houses and town halls. Jugglers, sleight-of-hand artists, acrobats, rope dancers, bear leaders, and fortunetellers, who belong to an ancient profession antedating recorded history, roamed the English countryside and regularly turned up at fairs and festivals. When performers of rude dramatic skits first appeared in England, no man can say. Mimes and clowns performing impromptu roles probably date from the Roman occupation. Certainly the clown has an ancient if not an honorable lineage. In the country, the mummers play and other types of folk drama go back to an early date.

The theatre proper, however, traces its origins back to the Church, even to the most solemn part of the liturgy, the Easter Mass. Between the ninth and the eleventh centuries throughout Europe the Easter Mass acquired richness and variety. In some churches, a brief text, or "trope," attached itself to the beginning portion of the Mass called the *Introit* and served as a kind of dramatic introduction to the service. In the Easter Mass this trope began, "*Quem quaeritis in sepulchro, O Christicolae?*" [Whom seek ye in the sepulchre, O followers of Christ?], and when the three Marys replied that they sought Jesus of Nazareth who had been crucified, the angel responded that he was not there, that they should go forth and say that he had risen as it had been prophesied. This bit of liturgical decoration gave rise to other dramatic episodes, notably to a similar playlet attached to the Christmas Mass. Liturgical drama of this type was acted throughout the European Church until the middle of the fifteenth century, by which time religious plays had already become secularized and had passed from the church into the streets and market place.

Precisely when or how this secularization came about, no one knows. A summer feast day, that of Corpus Christi, first established by the Church in 1264 and revived in 1311, provided an ideal time for an outdoor celebration and was soon the occasion for the performances of secularized Biblical plays. Since Corpus Christi Day falls on the Thursday after Trinity Sunday (the eighth Sunday after Easter), the performers could count on a long summer's day with a chance for good weather. In many towns throughout England on Corpus Christi Day associations of tradesmen known as guilds made themselves responsible for the presentation of cycles of plays based on the Bible, beginning with the Creation and ending with the Last Judgment. When possible, particular guilds chose plays that suited their callings. At Newcastle, York, and elsewhere, for example, the Shipwrights were responsible for the play concerned with building Noah's Ark. Corpus Christi Day was not the only occasion for the performance of guild plays. At Chester, for example, the plays were given during the week following Whitsunday. Although in some places the plays might be performed on stationary platforms, the general practice was to use "pageant wagons" —which in America would be called "floats"—platforms or structures on wheels which could go from place to place about the town until the whole cycle had been seen in sequence at several stations. When an entire cycle was given in one day, the performances had to start early and end late. The York cycle numbered at one time at least fifty plays, forty-eight of which have survived. If the audience tired of them, the records do not show it, and the cyclic plays, given in the language of the people, continued in popular esteem in some places until Shakespeare's time. Plays were acted at Chester in the 1570's and at Coventry, only a few miles from Stratford, until 1580.

These cyclic plays performed by the trade guilds are usually called miracle or mystery plays (the latter probably from an old French word for trade). Literary historians have sometimes tried to make a distinction between mystery and miracle plays. They would restrict mystery plays to those based on the Bible and miracle plays to those based on episodes in the lives of the saints, but the distinction has not gained currency, and both terms are used to describe the guild plays. Saints plays were

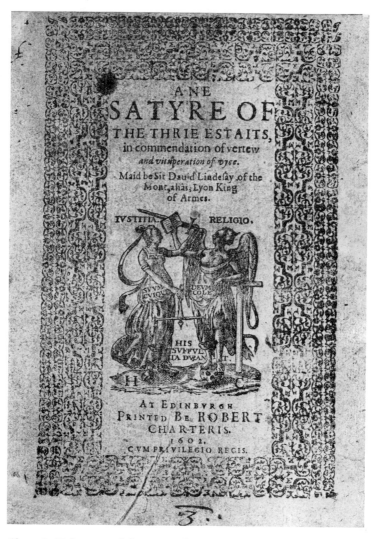

Plate 2. Title page of the 1602 edition of Sir David Lindsay's *Satire of the Three Estates.* Courtesy of the Huntington Library.

THE
TRAGEDIE OF GORBODVC,

whereof thzee Actes were wzytten by
Thomas Nortone, and the two laſte by
Thomas Sackuyle.
Sett foꝛthe as the ſame was ſhewed befoꝛe the
QVENES moſt excellent Maieſtie, in her highnes
Court of Whitehall, the.rviij.day of January,
Anno Domini. 1561. By the Gentlemen
of Thynner Temple in London.

IMPRYNTED AT LONDON
in Fleteſtrete, at the Signe of the
Faucon by *William Griffith:* And are
to be ſold at his Shop in Saincte
Dunſtones Churchyarde in
the Weſt of *London.*

Anno, 1565. Septemb.22. 23

Plate 3. Title page of the earliest English tragedy.

never so popular in England as in France and elsewhere on the Continent.

The significant fact about the guild plays in the growth of the dramatic tradition in England is their popularity over a great span of years and their dissemination throughout the country. As late as the mid-sixteenth century, even many small towns had a summer festival of drama in which large numbers of citizens participated. Gradually non-Biblical material crept into the stories, particularly in certain roles that offered possibilities for comedy. Noah had trouble getting his wife into the Ark, for instance, and had to beat her "black and blue" to the jollification of the spectators. The raging of King Herod became a comic scene, and the devils in the Last Judgment made much comic by-play as they snatched urchins from the street and carried them off to Hell Mouth. Finally, in a sheep-stealing episode in the Second Shepherds' Play in the Towneley (or Wakefield) Cycle, we have a fully developed comedy taken from the folklore of the countryside.

Still another type of drama, also religious in its beginnings, flourished in the fifteenth century. This was the morality play, an allegorical drama in which the characters are personified abstractions such as Envy, Pride, Mercy, Repentance, and the like. The conflict in this type of drama is between Good and Evil for the Soul of Man, with a variety of situations precipitated by such characters as the Seven Deadly Sins, who are opposed by the Seven Virtues.

The longest morality play (more than 3600 lines) and one of the most comprehensive in theme is *The Castle of Perseverance,* extant in a manuscript now in the Folger Library. Dating from about 1425, it exemplifies most of the situations found in this type of play. Human Kind, the hero, tempted by the World, the Flesh, and the Devil, takes refuge in the Castle of Perseverance, where he is besieged by the Seven Deadly Sins and defended by the Seven Virtues. Having grown old during a long war of words, Human Kind is tempted to leave the Castle by Covetousness, the sin peculiar to old age, but he soon repents, and after

Plate 4. Portrait of Richard Burbage. From an engraving in the Folger Library of the painting in Dulwich College.

Mercy, Truth, Justice, and Peace have delivered sermons, God the Father pardons Human Kind, and the play closes with advice to the audience to "think on your last ending."

The manuscript contains an interesting diagram showing the method of staging. A rough drawing of the Castle occupies the center of an arena with fixed scaffolds at intervals around the circumference for other scenes as they would be required. This multiple-set type of staging was common in the medieval drama and persisted to the Elizabethan period, particularly in plays at court. The audience conveniently forgot the other sets while action was taking place on the one required at the moment.

Despite the unpromising subject matter of the morality plays, they were popular in the second half of the fifteenth century and they continued in favor down to the accession of Queen Elizabeth. Indeed some belated moralities were acted during her reign, and morality play elements occasionally appear in the fully matured Elizabethan drama.

One reason for the popularity of the moralities was the amount of comedy that the actors managed to introduce. Even in so early a play as *The Castle of Perseverance* the personified abstractions were qualified slightly by the comic appearance of Belial, a devil equipped with bizarre fireworks. In the somewhat later play of *Mankind* (ca. 1475), the chief interest is in the clownery of Titivillus, the great devil, and his cohorts. At one point the comic characters Nought, New Guise, and Now-A-Days sing a travesty of a Christmas carol that must have delighted unsqueamish audiences, though a modern editor simply prints a series of dots and says, "The song is unprintable."

Mankind also illustrates the development of a professional class of actors. No longer is drama left to the auspices of clerks attached to religious establishments, to trade guilds, or to any other amateurs. As early as the last quarter of the fifteenth century town records in many parts of England show that professional actors were strolling from town to town with amusing plays in their repertories. In *Mankind* even the collection of money is made a scene of comedy as Titivillus passes his hat

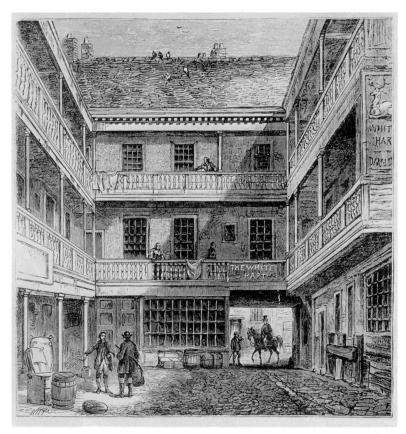

Plate 5. The yard of the White Hart Inn.   Before the erection of professional playhouses, the courtyards of inns like this provided a place where
actors could set up temporary stages. Spectators stood in the yard or sat in
the galleries.

and solicits the audience to pay. The most popular characters in the morality plays were the devils and their assistants. From an early date these comedians were responsible for the enduring popularity of theatrical performances throughout the country. During the half-century after *Mankind* professional troupes of actors multiplied, and during the reign of Henry VIII the country swarmed with players who acted out of doors or in manor houses, castles, and town halls to the increasing delight of the spectators.

A new type of play generally called an interlude developed in this period and gained popularity. The term is not precise and scholars debate about its meaning. Interludes were usually short dramatic pieces, frequently corresponding in length to a one-act play, and were often performed in the halls of great houses, sometimes as part of the entertainment offered at a dinner for some visiting dignitary. They were secular in tone, though some interludes continued to use personified abstractions of a sort. In one of the most curious of the type, *A New Interlude and a Merry of the Nature of the Four Elements*, attributed to John Rastell and written soon after the accession of Henry VIII, we are treated to a long dramatized lesson in science.

The more popular interludes, however, abandoned teaching in favor of sheer entertainment; the best of the writers in this kind was John Heywood, who provided short comic plays and farces for Henry VIII and his noblemen. Although Heywood was not an innovator and was content to borrow from Chaucer and to adapt French farcical stories to dramatic form, his interludes have a freshness and a vitality not found in morality plays with which they competed for favor. Among the better known of Heywood's interludes is the *Play of the Weather*, in which Jupiter decides to let people choose their own weather but has to return to arbitrary methods when no two can agree on what they want. Another of his interludes, the *Four P's*, exemplifies an ancient but still popular comic device, the contest to see who can tell the biggest lie.

Many interludes and belated morality plays on a wide variety of themes survive from the first half of the sixteenth century. They include political satires like John Skelton's *Magnificence* and Sir David Lindsay's *Satire of the Three Estates*, dramatized tracts concerned with religious controversy like John Bale's *God's Promises* and other works from his vitriolic pen, and plays entirely for entertainment like those of Heywood and such embryonic comedies as *Tom Tyler and His Wife*. The secular interludes made a significant contribution to the comic tradition, and the satiric moralities gave a new dramatic purpose to the stage. The somewhat amorphous drama of the early sixteenth century stimulated the continued development of a popular taste for plays.

The players of interludes did not confine their performances to the great halls of the nobility but often took to the road. Entries in the town records of the visits of players increased markedly in the 1530's and continued through the rest of the century. Scarcely a town was too small to have a visit from a group of strolling players, who frequently described themselves as the servants of some noble lord. This designation merely meant that the nobleman had consented to become the patron of the company of players and thus to lend them his name as a measure of protection against harassment from local authorities, for players occupied a low position in the social scale and were frequently classified in civic regulations with vagabonds and sturdy beggars, a situation that prevailed until Shakespeare's lifetime.

Although relics of the old types of drama cropped up now and then throughout the sixteenth century, by the early years of Elizabeth's reign mature secular drama had come into being. The earliest type to develop was comedy, partly because of a strong native tradition of comic stage situations and partly because the new learning of the Renaissance had familiarized academic audiences with Roman comedy. It was not mere chance that one of Shakespeare's earliest plays, *The Comedy of Errors*, was an adaptation from the *Menaechmi* of Plautus, for he may

Plate 6. An interior sketch of the Swan playhouse, made by Arend van Buchell from information supplied by Johannes de Witt in 1596.

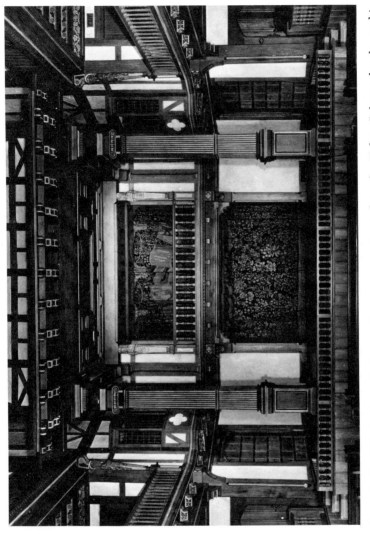

Plate 7. An Elizabethan playhouse stage as reconstructed in the Folger Library by the architect, Paul Cret. This stage is supposed to simulate the characteristic construction in the public theatres but it does not attempt to imitate any particular playhouse. Details of the balconies, inner stage, and the placement of entry doors are controversial.

have remembered the Roman dramatist from his grammar school studies. As early as 1553 Nicholas Udall, a former headmaster at Eton, composed a play on a Roman model and gave it the title of *Ralph Roister Doister*. Though it owes much to Plautine comedy, it is recognizably English in spirit. Sometime about 1553–1554, the students of Christ's College, Cambridge, saw performed in their college hall another English comedy, *Gammer Gurton's Needle* by an unidentified "Mr. S., Master of Arts." This play is still amusing enough to gain an audience.

On January 18, 1562, two years before Shakespeare was born, the young gentlemen of the Inner Temple, one of the Inns of Court where law students received their training, presented before Queen Elizabeth the first fully developed English tragedy of which we have record, *The Tragedy of Gorboduc*. The authors, Thomas Sackville, later Earl of Dorset, and Thomas Norton, modeled their play after the style of the Roman writer Seneca but they also showed a familiarity with Italian dramatists. Though Elizabethan drama had not yet reached full maturity, the forms of both tragedy and comedy were now established and the development of both types would show rapid progress during the next three decades to culminate in the work of Shakespeare and his contemporaries.

The growing demand for plays and the development of full-length drama had created such a need for professional playhouses by the late 1570's that in 1576 a cabinetmaker-turned-actor named James Burbage erected the first building in London designed exclusively for the use of players. To it he gave the descriptive name, The Theatre. Its site was east of Finsbury Fields, a park area to the northward of the city proper, on land leased from one Giles Alleyn. Burbage had been careful to choose a site just outside the jurisdiction of the city authorities yet close enough to be accessible to playgoers. Within a year another playhouse called the Curtain (from the name of the estate on which it was located) opened nearby. London now had two professional public playhouses, both outside the city's jurisdiction. It was important to be beyond the reach of the

Plate 8. The Bear Garden, the Rose, and the Globe. A detail from the background of an equestrian portrait of King James by Delaram. The view of London was supposed to represent the city as it was when James came to the throne in 1603.

aldermen of London, for they maintained an inveterate hostility to the players on the grounds that they caused disturbances, brought together crowds that spread the plague, lured apprentices from their work, and were generally ungodly.

An early attempt to open a playhouse within the city was made by Richard Farrant, Master of the Children of Windsor Chapel. For a long time the choirboys of Windsor Chapel, like the choirboys of the Chapel Royal and St. Paul's Cathedral, had been accustomed to performing plays and to taking part in other entertainments at Court. Farrant conceived the notion of renting a hall in part of the old Blackfriars Monastery and of fitting it up for a playhouse on the pretext of rehearsing plays to be performed before the Queen. Although the Blackfriars property was within the walls of the city of London, not far from St. Paul's Cathedral, it retained its ancient exemption from the jurisdiction of the city's aldermen. Even so, Farrant did not dare try to open a public theatre but announced that it would be a "private" house though open to paying customers. This distinction between "public" and "private" theatres would persist throughout the Elizabethan period. Farrant's subterfuge worked and he opened his playhouse late in 1576 or early in 1577. Despite trouble with his landlord his theatre was a modest success until his death in 1580. The Blackfriars Theatre operated for another four years under the direction of William Hunnis, Master of the Children of the Chapel Royal, with the help for a time of John Lyly, a young novelist and dramatist. There Lyly's own plays were performed by the boy actors.

From the time of the opening of the earliest formal theatres, the public and the private houses differed widely in physical characteristics and methods of staging. The public theatres, for all we know, may have been influenced in their shape and construction by the circular arenas, like those on the Bankside across the Thames, which were used for bull- and bear-baiting. A more significant influence on their architecture, however, came from the inns. Long before the erection of regular theatres, players had used the yards of inns, and in London certain inns

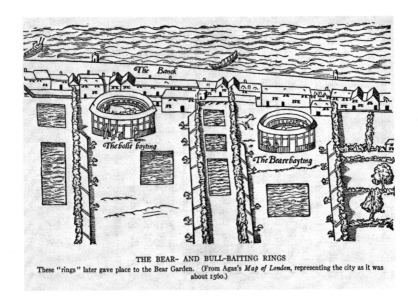

THE BEAR- AND BULL-BAITING RINGS

These "rings" later gave place to the Bear Garden. (From Agas's *Map of London*, representing the city as it was about 1560.)

Plate 9. Bear and Bull Rings. From Agas' *Map of London* as reproduced in J. Q. Adams, *Shakespearean Playhouses* (Boston, 1917), p. 123.

in building the Rose playhouse, not far from the Bear Garden. Henslowe has earned the gratitude of literary historians because he kept an account book, usually described as his "Diary," which preserves much theatrical and dramatic history. His son-in-law Edward Alleyn was one of the most famous actors and stage managers of the day.

The popularity of Henslowe's Rose stimulated another businessman, Francis Langley, goldsmith, to purchase the Manor of Paris Garden, west of the site of the Rose and the Bear Garden. There he erected in 1595 a new theatre which he called the Swan. This playhouse is of interest to historians because in 1596 a Dutch priest, Johannes de Witt, saw a performance at the Swan and described the stage to a friend, Arend van Buchell, who made a drawing that is the earliest visual representation of an Elizabethan stage in use.

Because of its association with Shakespeare, the best known of the Bankside theatres is the Globe. The Globe was erected in 1599, in part from timbers of The Theatre, which the lessees, Cuthbert and Richard Burbage, moved across the Thames on December 28, 1598, to a site in Maiden Lane which they had chosen when their landlord made trouble over the lease of The Theatre. To be owners of the new playhouse, the Burbages organized a stock company consisting of themselves and four actors including Shakespeare and John Heminges, who was later to be one of the editors of the 1623 collection of Shakespeare's plays. The theatre owners, or "house-keepers" as they were then called, received half the receipts from the galleries. The acting company received the other half and all the receipts taken at the door. Thus Shakespeare, who was a house-keeper, a member of the acting company, and a dramatist, received income from all three sources. The Globe was completed in 1599 and lasted until 1613, when it burned down after a piece of wadding from a cannon fired during a performance of *Henry VIII* ignited its thatched roof. A second Globe was soon erected to take its place. The first Globe is usually pictured as octagonal on the outside, but despite the octagonal pictures in seventeenth-cen-

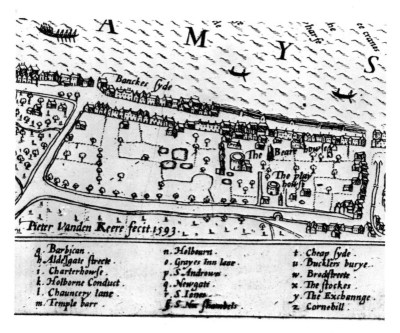

Plate 10. John Norden's Map. Reproduced from *Speculum Britanniae*
(1593).

like the Cross Keys, the Bell, and the Bull were noted as playing places for professional actors. At the inns, the players had been accustomed to set up a stage at one end of the open courtyard and to accommodate spectators in the courtyard, which was open to the weather, and in the surrounding galleries.

The public theatres for many years retained this open-courtyard feature. There the "groundlings" for the price of a penny could stand while more opulent spectators could pay a higher fee for the privilege of sitting in the galleries. Plays were performed in the daytime, beginning in the early afternoon, for the stage had no means of artificial lighting. The public theatres could not be used in the worst weather or in the dead of winter. The private houses were enclosed halls in which plays could be given at night. They could be used in winter and in all weathers. The stage was lighted by candles, lamps, or torches. The private houses were not private in the sense of restricting audiences to any special groups but prices were higher than in the public playhouses, a fact that may have given the private houses a somewhat more select audience.

A place of recreation long popular with the citizens of London was the Bankside, an extensive area on the Southwark side of the Thames and west of what is now Southwark Cathedral. Much of this territory consisted of land that had formerly belonged to the Church or the Crown, and the aldermen of London had no authority over certain areas like the Manor of Paris Garden and the Liberty of the Clink. These and other localities beyond the jurisdiction of the city became the sites for a variety of amusements.

To the Bankside, Londoners went to witness bear- and bull-baitings at arenas erected for the purpose. After one of the old arenas collapsed in 1583 with some loss of life, a polygonal amphitheatre called the New Bear Garden was erected. Other even less savory enticements brought Londoners to the Bankside. This area by the 1580's was attracting the interest of theatrical entrepreneurs. One of these was Philip Henslowe, a semiliterate but shrewd businessman, who in 1587 was instrumental tury views of London, some evidence points to a circular shape. The interior may have been circular. The Globe was the model for the Fortune Theatre, which Henslowe and Alleyn erected in 1600 north of the city on the opposite side of Finsbury Fields from the site of The Theatre and the Curtain. In only one essential did they change the design. The Fortune was square. The builder's specifications for the Fortune, which have survived, provide the best existing information about Elizabethan theatrical construction.

A playhouse that combined the functions of a theatre with those of an arena for bear- and bull-baiting was the Hope, erected in 1613 on the site of the Bear Garden, which had fallen into decay and was torn down to make way for the new building. The owners of the Hope were Philip Henslowe and a partner, Jacob Meade. The contract which the partners signed with the carpenter-contractor exists and throws some light on its construction. The Hope had a portable stage which could be removed when the building was required for other purposes. Over the stage area was a permanent canopy. But details of the construction of the stage and the entry doors that we would like to have are omitted. The contract specifies that the contractor is to build the Hope "of such large compass, form, wideness, and height as the playhouse called the Swan."

One other public theatre needs to be mentioned. This was the Red Bull, built about 1605 in the upper end of St. John's Street, Clerkenwell, about a mile from the old Curtain. This theatre was a favorite with London apprentices and was the place where some of the more boisterous of Elizabethan plays were performed.

Almost as important as the Globe in the history of Shakespeare's company was the second Blackfriars Theatre. In 1596 James Burbage purchased a portion of the Frater building in the rambling old Blackfriars Monastery and remodeled it for a theatre. Like the earlier Blackfriars, it was a covered hall, but it was more elaborately designed, with galleries for spectators and a better equipped stage at one end. The precise construc-

22

Plate 11. Portrait of Edward Alleyn. From an engraving in the Folger Library of the portrait in Dulwich College.

Plate 12. The Swan playhouse. A detail from Visscher's engraving of 1616, reproduced from the copy belonging to the London Topographical Society.

24

tion of the stage we do not know. Burbage leased the theatre for several years to the managers of the boy actors of the Chapel Royal, but in 1608, when the lease expired, a syndicate of seven actors, including Shakespeare, took it over. Henceforth Shakespeare's company operated the Blackfriars as a "private" theatre, but in actuality it was the playhouse regularly used by the company in winter.

Both the Blackfriars and the Globe stages, like other Elizabethan stages, were platform stages without the familiar proscenium arch of the modern theatre and of course without a curtain to come down between the acts and at the end of the play. These stages also lacked painted and movable scenery, though Elizabethan theatres made considerably more use of stage properties than we have been led to believe. The question that has aroused the greatest controversy concerns the use of an inner stage and the location of entry doors and balconies in the back of the stage. The Swan drawing shows a projecting platform stage with two doors flat against the rear wall. People, presumably spectators, are shown in the balcony over the rear stage doors. The Swan drawing also shows a canopy supported by columns over a portion of the stage and a room above that. The canopy and room above were characteristics of the public theatres. The upper room, called the "tiring house," was used for dressing and storage. From a trap door in the canopy, called the "heavens," gods and angels might descend when the action required it.

Most modern reconstructions of the stage of the Globe provide an inner stage, useful for bedroom or "study" scenes, with an upper stage above it. Both of these are closed with curtains. Stage doors open obliquely on each side with boxes or balconies above. This type of construction would best suit a scene like the balcony scene in *Romeo and Juliet*. Some scholars insist that the inner stage was too deeply recessed to permit many in the audience to see properly and that bedroom scenes must have been staged farther forward on the platform, with properties brought into use as they were required. There is no convincing evidence that the regular Elizabethan theatres were designed for performances in the round. There is much evidence for the use of an inner and upper stage with entry doors set either flat against the back or diagonally on the sides. It should be pointed out, however, that the text and directions of many plays seem to indicate the use of the main stage for scenes that editors like to relegate to an inner stage. Such use of the main stage suggests that necessary properties and equipment could be set up in advance and ignored by the audience until time for their use, as in the simultaneous-stage settings in medieval drama.

Where there are so many suggestions of both types of staging, one cannot escape the conclusion that usage varied and that stage construction in the theatres may have differed in some important details. Actors have always been skilled in improvising, and Elizabethan players had to be unusually adroit in this respect in order to adapt their plays to a wide variety of conditions: performances in the great hall at Court, in a public theatre in the daytime, in a private theatre at night, or on some makeshift stage in a country town when the plague closed the London theatres and sent them strolling through the provinces.

During Shakespeare's lifetime the principal theatres were occupied by companies of actors organized under the patronage of various titled personages. The company with which Shakespeare was associated for most of his active career had for its earliest patron, Henry Carey, Lord Hunsdon, the Lord Chamberlain. Hence they were known as the Lord Chamberlain's Men. After the accession of James I, the King became their patron and they were known as the King's Men. They were the great rivals of the Lord Admiral's Men, managed by Henslowe and Alleyn. Competitors with all the adult companies were the child actors drawn from the choirboys of the Chapel Royal, Windsor, and St. Paul's. These actors are referred to in *Hamlet* as "an aery of children, little eyases, that cry out on the top of question, and are most tyrannically clapped for't." The adult companies recruited some of their best impersonators of female roles from the children's companies, for the Elizabethan stage

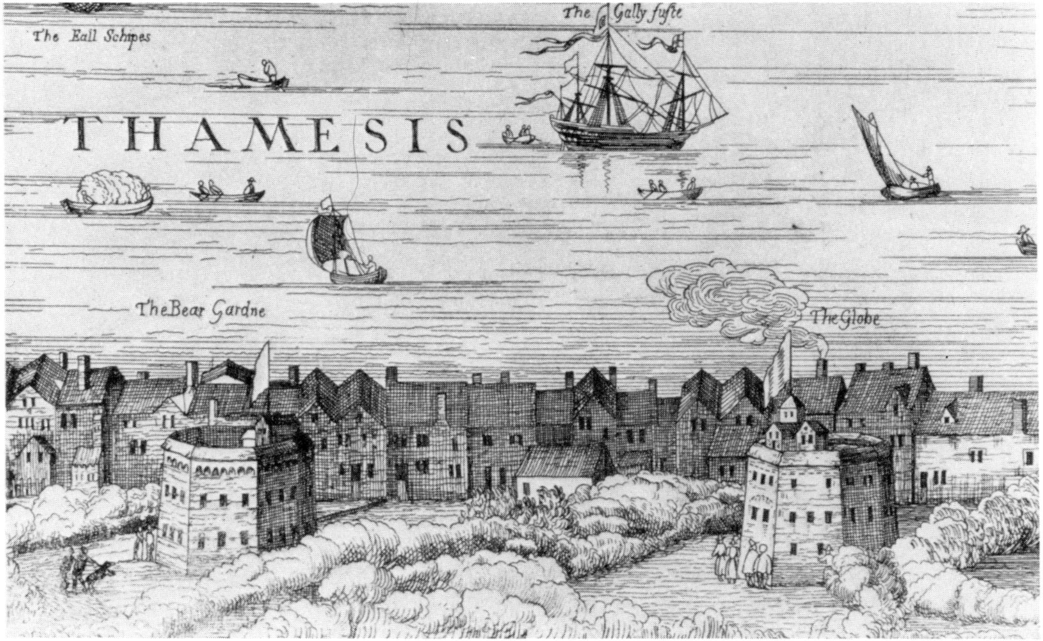
The Eall Schipes
The Gally fuste
THAMESIS
The Bear Gardne
The Globe

Plate 13. The Bear Garden and the Globe. A detail from Visscher's engraving of 1616, reproduced from the copy belonging to the London Topographical Society.

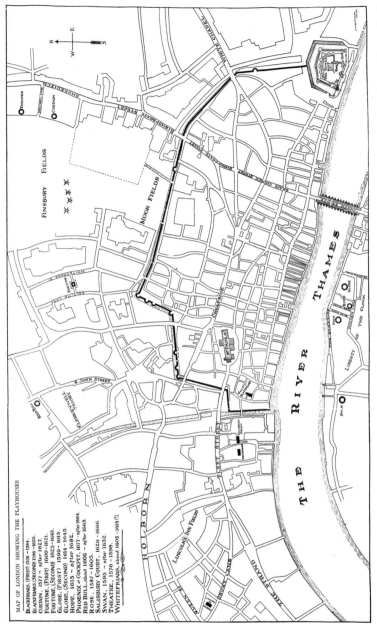

MAP OF LONDON SHOWING THE PLAYHOUSES

BLACKFRIARS, (FIRST) 1576 - 1584.
BLACKFRIARS, (SECOND) 1596 - 1655.
CURTAIN, 1577 - after 1627.
FORTUNE, (FIRST) 1600 - 1621.
FORTUNE, (SECOND) 1623 - 1661.
GLOBE, (FIRST) 1599 - 1613.
GLOBE, (SECOND) 1614 - 1645.
HOPE, 1613 - after 1682.
PHŒNIX or COCKPIT, 1617 - after 1664.
RED BULL, about 1605 - after 1663.
ROSE, 1587 - 1605.
SALISBURY COURT, 1629 - 1666.
SWAN, 1595 - after 1632.
THEATRE, 1576 - 1598.
WHITEFRIARS, about 1605 - 1614 (?).

28

Plate 14. Sites of the playhouses. The heavy black line indicates the old wall of the City of London. From J. Q. Adams, *Shakespearean Playhouses* (Boston, 1917).

never employed women as players. That innovation had to wait until the Restoration.

Elizabethan acting must have been skillful and effective. To hold the attention of a restless and unruly audience in close proximity, the actors had to speak their lines well and simulate their parts to perfection. The impersonation of women's roles by boys seems to us the least satisfactory element in Elizabethan acting, but there is ample evidence that youths succeeded in these parts. No Elizabethan complained that a boy spoiled the role of Juliet.

Elizabethan audiences were not accustomed to the conventions of modern staging and did not expect realistic stage sets and colorful scenery in the professional playhouses. At Court, it is true, the masques were mounted with magnificent splendor —and at great cost—but these were spectacles for royalty, and few who witnessed plays in the theatres ever saw a masque. We have perhaps overemphasized the bareness of the Elizabethan stage and we may forget that Elizabethan producers made adequate use of stage properties. Nevertheless we are correct in insisting that Elizabethan plays were written primarily for the ear rather than the eye. It was not always necessary to stick up a board reading "The Forest of Arden" or other locale. The poetry frequently conveyed the description adequately for the audience to comprehend both the place and the atmosphere that the dramatist wanted to suggest. In the age of Shakespeare poetic drama reached its greatest height, and one can speculate as to whether Shakespeare would have written so vividly if he could have left to the carpenter and the scene painter the effects that he achieved in words.

Plate 15. The stage of the Globe as illustrated in the John C. Adams model.

SUGGESTED READING

Detailed discussion of the development of the English stage in the periods covered may be found in the following monumental works: E. K. Chambers, *The Medieval Stage* (2 vols., Oxford, 1903); E. K. Chambers, *The Elizabethan Stage* (4 vols., Oxford, 1923); and Gerald E. Bentley, *The Jacobean and Caroline Stage* (5 vols., Oxford, 1941–1956). Detailed treatment of the drama will be found in Karl Young, *The Drama of the Medieval Church* (2 vols., Oxford, 1933) and F. E. Schelling, *Elizabethan Drama, 1558–1642* (2 vols., Boston, 1908). Hardin Craig, *English Religious Drama of the Middle Ages* (Oxford, 1955) will be serviceable to the specialist rather than to the general reader. A sound and scholarly work is Wilhelm Creizenach, *The English Drama in the Age of Shakespeare* (London, 1916). Brief but useful are F. S. Boas, *An Introduction to Tudor Drama* (Oxford, 1933), C. F. Tucker Brooke, *The Tudor Drama* (Boston, 1911), and F. S. Boas, *An Introduction to Stuart Drama* (Oxford, 1946). E. K. Chambers, *The English Folk-Play* (Oxford, 1933) provides an excellent summary of information on this subject. Informal and readable is W. Bridges-Adams, *The Irresistible Theatre: Vol. I. From the Conquest to the Commonwealth* (London, 1957). Information about the status of actors and the organization of actor companies may be found in T. W. Baldwin, *The Organization and Personnel of the Shakespearean Company* (Princeton, 1927).

The most complete history of the Elizabethan theatres is Joseph Q. Adams, *Shakespearean Playhouses* (Boston, 1917). A useful survey of theatrical history with helpful illustrations is Allardyce Nicoll, *The Development of the Theatre* (London, 1927). Valuable for its

31

discussion of the English heritage from the classical past is Lily B. Campbell, *Scenes and Machines on the English Stage During the Renaissance: A Classical Revival* (Cambridge, 1923). Valuable information on theatrical practices is available in George F. Reynolds, *The Staging of Elizabethan Plays at the Red Bull Theater, 1605–1625* (New York, 1940). An elaborate discussion of the construction of the Globe Theatre will be found in John C. Adams, *The Globe Playhouse: Its Design and Equipment* (Cambridge, Mass., 1942). A model of the Globe made by Mr. Adams and Mr. Irwin Smith is on exhibition in the Folger Library, and a description with scale drawings and pictures is available in Irwin Smith, *Shakespeare's Globe Playhouse: A Modern Reconstruction* (New York, 1956). Another scholar's conception of the construction of the Globe is C. Walter Hodges, *The Globe Restored: A Study of the Elizabethan Theatre* (London, 1953). Students interested in the practical aspects of staging a play on an Elizabethan type of stage will find helpful Richard Southern, *The Open Stage and the Modern Theatre in Research and Practice* (London, 1953).

The literature on the physical aspects of the Elizabethan theatres and the influence of structural features on the drama is extensive and some of it is controversial. An informative book is W. J. Lawrence, *The Physical Conditions of the Elizabethan Public Playhouse* (Cambridge, Mass., 1927). Mr. Lawrence was the author of various articles and monographs giving his views of stage construction. Useful also is Thornton Shirley Graves, *The Court and the London Theatres During the Reign of Queen Elizabeth* (Menasha, Wis., 1913). Collateral information is available in Alfred Harbage, *Shakespeare's Audience* (New York, 1941); Arthur C. Sprague, *Shakespeare and the Audience* (Cambridge, Mass., 1935) and *Shakespearian Players and Performances* (Cambridge, Mass., 1953). Further bibliographical clues to a study of the theatres are available in Allardyce Nicoll, "Studies in the Elizabethan Stage Since 1900," *Shakespeare Survey I* (1948), 1–16.

One of the most concise and helpful discussions of the vexed problems concerning the Elizabethan stage is to be found in a lecture by F. P. Wilson, delivered at the University of Amsterdam and published in *Neophilologus* as No. 28 of the Allard Pierson Lectures under the title of "The Elizabethan Theatre" (Groningen, 1955).

Plate 16. The title page of William Alabaster's *Roxana* (1632), showing a platform stage with what appears to be a curtained inner stage.

A Note on the Views of London and the Theatres

The question of the validity of the various contemporary "Views of London" by engravers and map-makers is too complicated for discussion in such a brief space. The matter is treated in detail in I. A. Shapiro, "The Bankside Theatres: Early Engravings," *Shakespeare Survey I* (1948), 25–37, and by Irwin Smith, *Shakespeare's Globe Playhouse*, (New York, 1956), pp. 14–28. Mr. Shapiro argues from the evidence in the engravings that the Globe was round on the outside. Mr. Smith, from similar evidence in addition to other evidence presented by J. C. Adams, argues that the Globe was octagonal. Some views show it as an octagonal structure; others show a round exterior. Since artists and engravers were free in their interpretation of topographical details and borrowed from one another, one can never be certain of the accuracy of these illustrations.

Plate 17. The Swan (39), the Bear Garden (38), and the Globe (37); St. Paul's Cathedral, as it was before the Great Fire of 1666, appears in the background. From Merian's *View of London*, 1638. From a copy in the Folger Library.